TREESPIRITEDWOMAN

COLLEEN
BALDRICA

BEAVER'S
POND
PRESS

Photographs by Jim Baldrica

ISBN-13: 978-159298-144-1

Library of Congress Catalog Number: 2006923340

Printed in the United States of America

Sixth Printing: 2014

19 18 17 16 15 14   6 7 8 9 10 11

BEAVER'S
POND
PRESS

7108 Ohms Lane
Edina, MN 55439
(952) 829-8818
www.BeaversPondPress.com

To order, visit *www.BeaversPondBooks.com*
or call 1-800-901-3480. Reseller discounts available.

To the memory of my Grandmother,

To my Mother, whom I've come to cherish,

And to all my Sisters across the world,

This book is written for you.

"Let Go and Trust."

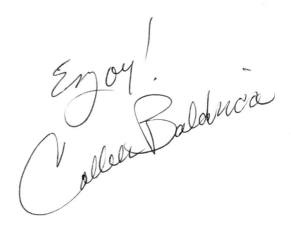

TABLEOFCONTENTS

Acknowledgements

T hank you to my earliest readers for their friendship, support, and encouragement; love and appreciation to my husband, who has been my constant supporter; and endless gratitude to my editor, Nancy Baldrica.

Prologue

My mother's mother lived with us while I was growing up. Grandmother was about four foot ten, round around the middle, dyed her hair a blue gray, and wore Lilies of the Valley cologne. She was half Chippewa (Ojibwe) and half French Canadian. When Grandmother was young, she and her six sisters were told they must attend the Indian Boarding School on the White Earth Indian Reservation in northern Minnesota. They left their home and their parents, and rarely returned until they were adults. During the summers, Grandmother and her sisters would stay with different families and do housekeeping. I once asked Grandmother why she and her sisters didn't go home during the summer. She said it was easier for everyone if they didn't, and changed the subject.

Whenever I asked Grandmother about life on the reservation and attending the boarding school, all she would tell me was that she played on the basketball team and they were very good. When I asked more questions, Grandmother would say it was a long time ago, and then she'd talk about something else. She never wanted to talk about her past and I never pushed. If I had it to do over, I would get her to talk more about her life and her Native American heritage, and share her stories that are now lost to me.

As a child, I used to think it was strange that Grandmother insisted her grandchildren be registered on the Indian rolls. I'm five foot six, thin built, with blue eyes and blond hair. No one looking at me would ever imagine that I'm officially recorded by the Minnesota Chippewa Tribe as a Native American from the White Earth Reservation, Pembina Band. As an adult, I'm glad that my grandmother insisted on putting us on the Indian rolls. I treasure that part of my ancestry.

I was always closer to my grandmother than my mother. Grandmother never raised her voice to me, and she always shared her rules for life, such as: "Always wash your hands when you get up because you don't know what they touched while you were asleep." I always thought my grandmother was the wisest woman I knew.

Grandmother would take me on long walks through the woods and would tell me stories. I loved listening to her talk. As we would walk, she would point out trees, and she loved to see hawks circle above. We would find a place to sit, listen to the sounds around us, and try to identify all we were hearing. I loved that game.

Grandmother died of a massive heart attack the year I was twenty-three. It was shortly after my husband decided he didn't want to be married. I felt so lost and alone. In just a couple of short months, I had lost my marriage, and my confidant and encourager. I could tell Grandmother anything, and she would never judge me. She believed in me, even when I didn't believe in myself.

Six months after Grandmother died, my mother called me and asked if I'd help clean out my grandmother's room. As I sat on my grandmother's bed, going through her old, blue jewelry box, tears fell down my cheeks. I held her rosary in my fingers and thought of the times I had gone to mass with her. I remembered her telling me, "God doesn't care where you go to worship, it's just important that you do." I wasn't raised Catholic, or even in a church. I knew it upset my grandmother that my parents didn't practice some religion. I guess my mom had her reasons for not wanting to go to church. I just didn't know what they were, and they were never a topic of discussion.

Grandmother had a cedar chest that was always locked. As I slipped the key into the lock, something moved inside me, and I felt a twinge of apprehension. I was entering into my grandmother's private world, and I didn't know what to expect. I opened the lid and first saw an old handmade shawl. It was off-white in color and made of delicate lace. I didn't remember seeing it before, but it was lovely. There were old picture albums and important papers, like her marriage license. Seeing the marriage license made me smile. I didn't remember my grandfather; he died when I was just three years old. Grandmother once told me she wasn't afraid to die, because then she would be with Grandpa again. Under some handmade doilies, there was a book. As I took it out and opened it, I realized it was a journal.

I sat down on the floor and began to read. The first page said, "This journal is my gift to Little One. May it help you with life's lessons long after I am gone." Little One was a secret name Grandmother called me. Realizing Grandma meant for me to have this journal, I said nothing about the book to Mom. It was too special and personal, and I didn't want to share it with anyone at that moment. I quietly placed the journal in my bag to take home, where I could read it in the privacy of my bedroom.

Grandmother loved to write. She always said, "Stories are a part of lives, and I believe that God meant for us to share these stories."

When I got home that evening, I opened the journal again. The first page was dedicated to me, and the second page was a personal letter. The rest of the journal was blank. I read Grandmother's letter.

Dear Little One,

When you read this I will be dead. I want you to know I am not afraid of death. Life has been good to me, and I am ready. You are young, and have your whole life ahead of you. I want you to know how proud I am of you, and I feel blessed whenever I can tell people you are my granddaughter. You possess many strengths and talents that are obvious to others. Now it is up to you to recognize these gifts within yourself. There will be people put in your life to share their wisdom and knowledge. Listen to what they have to say. Go explore life, and don't be afraid to take risks.

Little One, you're probably asking yourself why I would leave you a journal. I know you told me you don't like to write, but I believe someday this journal will have a purpose. When the time is right, you will know what you are to write to fill these pages. This journal is my special gift to you. Always remember, you are loved.

Your Loving Grandmother.

When I finished reading the letter, tears were streaming down my cheeks. I reread the letter a number of times, each time taking in all of my grandmother's words and wishing for more.

Grandmother was right when she said I would wonder about that journal. At the time, I didn't understand how important her gift would become. Yet a few years later, after meeting a very wise woman, it became clear: that journal was to become this book that is now in your hands.

ONE

Beginning

I first met her while hiking through the woods behind the college. She was old even then. Her face was lined from years of laughter, sun, and wind. Her light-brown eyes held flecks of gold, and I remember thinking she could see deep into my soul. I felt she knew my life and my thoughts. Her smile was very special. It brightened up her face, causing her eyes to sparkle. It was the moment I first saw that smile that I felt she could be trusted totally. Our unique relationship had begun.

I was in my third year of college and I loved to hike in the woods behind the school, especially in the fall. The leaves seemed to shout out. Their colors were so loud and glorious. Whenever I walked the woods, I felt at peace.

This particular fall day, while hiking deep in the woods, I stopped to rest by a grove of white birch trees. The trees seemed to be growing in a circular formation. It was then I noticed her, sitting on the ground, cross-legged, in the middle of the birch grove. Worried I had stumbled upon someone's private moment, I slowly turned and started to walk quietly away. That's when she said, *"Wait. Do not go. I was expecting you."*

I stopped, looked around, and saw no one else. I looked at her. She was still sitting on the ground, but now she was looking directly at me as if she expected me to join her. For a moment I was startled, yet there was something so familiar about her that I had to ask, "Do I know you?"

"Not at this time," she answered in a voice that sounded much like my grandmother's. It was a voice deeper than that of the average woman, yet it had a soft quality that made me want to lean near to listen.

My uneasiness with the situation must have been obvious. She smiled the most beautiful, calming smile, and patted the spot beside her. There was no doubt she expected me to sit beside her. When I look back on that day, I'm still not sure what really happened. I just know that I soon found myself sitting cross-legged on the ground next to a strange woman, and it seemed to be the exact place that I was meant to be.

We sat together in silence for what seemed to be a long while. The need to know her overwhelmed me, not just her name, but her thoughts and her feelings. It was such a strong sensation that I knew this meeting was not a coincidence. She had said she was expecting me, but why?

"What's your name?" I finally asked.

"*I have had many names, but I am now called Tree Spirited Woman,*" she answered quietly.

I didn't want to be rude, yet I wanted to ask what other names she'd had, and how she had gotten the name 'Tree Spirited Woman.' As I sat there thinking these thoughts, she smiled and said, "*The other names are not important. If you would like to listen, I will tell you how the name 'Tree Spirited Woman' was given to me.*"

I was sure I hadn't spoken. How did she know what I was thinking? As I looked at her, confused, a calmness spread over me. It was at that moment I realized I was to hear her stories, but before I could ask her another question, she began.

"I was younger then, and, much like you, I always loved to walk in the woods. It was a healthy woods, very much like this one. It, too, was filled with many different plants and trees.

"I was not always so trusting. It was a time in my life when I was feeling much emotional pain, as well as questioning which spiritual path to follow. While I walked, I talked aloud to my God. I was questioning my faith and what to do with my life. Finding myself deeper in the woods than I had ever traveled before, I felt the need to stop and listen. As I looked around, I found myself next to a large oak tree. I stood there, feeling the tree's heartbeat. It was not like your heartbeat or mine. It was a like a river flowing in the middle of the tree, much like the veins in one's body. I was unsure what to do next.

"Closing my eyes, I prayed to my God as I had never prayed before. 'What am I to do in this lifetime?' I asked. I heard not a voice but a clear thought telling me to lift my branches, for I must learn to let go. Unexpectedly, my arms slowly began to rise, as if they had a mind of their own. I could feel my hands gnarl, much like the limbs of a tree. Not opening my eyes, I stood very still and listened.

"The voice was speaking to me, now saying,

'You must be like the tree and trust in Me. I will take care of all your needs. See how I give the tree a time to rest. That time is called winter. It is a time for one to reflect and relax. When the time is right, the tree is given a new beginning. This is called spring, it is a time to try new ideas and take risks. Summer is a time of being. There may be some storms and pain, but, mostly, it is a time to just be content with where one is in life. There is always celebration in one's life, a time to be happy and shout out to others. For a tree, this season is autumn.

'It is important for you to become as trusting as the tree. Your seasons may not be as clear, but, still, they are there. It is now time for you to begin your new journey. You will gain much knowledge, and if you listen to all you meet, you will gain much wisdom. But first, you must let go of the pain you carry within yourself. There can be no growth until you let go and trust. Whichever spiritual path you chose to follow, I will be with you.'

"I was still standing with my eyes closed and my arms raised high in the air, feeling all my pain and doubts being pulled up through my body and out my fingertips. The voice continued.

'You will be known by many names, but 'Tree Spirited Woman' is the name I give to you. Use it wisely, and when it is time, pass on the lessons you have learned.'

"I stood for what seemed to be a long while before I opened my eyes. There was a peace within me like nothing I had ever felt before. I knew then my life would not be the same." The woman paused, looked into my eyes and said, *"That was how I was given the name 'Tree Spirited Woman.'*

"Since that time," she continued, *"I have lived many years, learned much knowledge, and gained an abundance of wisdom. My years are almost over. It is now time to pass on what I have learned to others."*

The story fascinated me, but it had created more questions. "How did you know I was coming?" I asked her.

"You saw me sitting in the grove of trees, waiting. I did not see you coming, but I knew you were there, and that you were the one."

"The one for what?" I asked, not understanding.

"You are the one to pass on the life lessons I have learned. For now, you are to listen. When it is time, you will share what I have said with others."

"What exactly am I to share?" I asked.

"Some might call them stories, fantasies, or even prophecies. I am not to say how one might interpret my message. It is for the listener, alone, to decide. I will talk mostly to women, as I am a woman, and I know women best. But what I will share will be good for men to know, as well. I will tell you what I know to be true, and it will be up to you to pass it on. Our paths have been connected."

Panic started to fill me. I was sure this woman had gotten me mixed up with someone else. I remember wanting to explain to her that someone else would be coming soon, and it would be her responsibility to pass on Tree Spirited Woman's truths.

She looked at me intensely and continued, *"You are the one. The gift of writing is within you, and it will make itself known in time. What I have to say is important. Women are questioning. Trust what I say. When it is time, the words will be given to you. Do not worry."*

"What is it that I am to tell women?" I asked.

"*There will be much information. I will meet with you in these woods in the early afternoon on the 28th of every month. We will sit, and I will share my knowledge with you. I will know if you are not coming. But that will not happen. You will be here.*"

"How many months will we meet?" I questioned.

She looked at me, smiled, and said patiently, "*We will meet for as long as needed. Our first meeting is now over. I am tired and have talked much. We will meet again on the 28th, in one month's time. It is now time for you to leave.*"

As I slowly stood, I looked down at Tree Spirited Woman. For a moment our eyes locked, then I turned and walked away, my mind turning with what had just occurred and what was to take place in these woods.

TWO

Reflections

All the way home, I thought about my meeting with Tree Spirited Woman, how she'd been given the name 'Tree Spirited Woman', and about how she had prayed as she had never prayed before. But mostly, I thought about how she expected me to write and share her words with others.

After entering the door of my house, life, as I knew it, resumed. My inner thoughts were pushed aside by the everyday tasks of caring for my son and daughter. That night, however, as I lay awake in my bed, I thought about Tree Spirited Woman again. Her words reminded me of what my grandmother had written: "There will be people put in your life to share their knowledge and wisdom. Listen to what they have to say"'.

I wondered if Grandmother had sent Tree Spirited Woman to me. Thinking of Grandmother in the silence of my bedroom made me miss her so deeply. The tears started to flow again. I felt so alone and uncertain."

I wanted to confide in someone about my encounter, but I couldn't think of anyone I could trust. I didn't want anyone trying to talk me out of meeting with Tree Spirited Woman, or worse, insisting on going with me.

That night, in bed, I decided to keep Tree Spirited Woman a secret, at least for the time being. I also decided to meet with her each month. I couldn't explain it, but I knew these meetings were going to be an important part of my life.

For the next couple of weeks, thoughts of Tree Spirited Woman kept popping into my head. I would be in the grocery store, and suddenly think of her smiling at me. At school, daydreams of her sitting in the woods filled dull moments.

One night in a dream, Grandmother came and talked to me. I don't remember her words, but she was carrying something in her hand that looked like a book, and a hawk was flying above her head.

When I awoke, I remember feeling peaceful. I still hadn't written anything in the journal she had left me. Nothing had seemed significant enough to write in this special book. In the morning, however, I knew exactly what I was going to do. As my coffee was brewing, I took out the journal. From that point on, the journal would be used to record my thoughts and the information Tree Spirited Woman passed on during our meetings. I decided I would write something about her each month, and, when the time was right, I would share her words with others.

September 30

Grandmother,

I have decided to start using your journal. It makes me smile thinking about how happy you'd be that I'm finally filling these pages.

I met a woman in the woods and I'm going to be writing about her. Her name is Tree Spirited Woman. She's interesting and kind of reminds me of you. She wants to meet with me once a month. I'm not sure how I'll find the time, between raising my children, going to school, and working part-time. But for some reason, it seems right.

THREE

Listening

On the 28th of the next month, I went back into the woods. There was a part of me that kept saying I didn't have the time to get involved with anything more. Yet, another part of me knew that going back was exactly what I was supposed to do. The truth is, I'd thought about Tree Spirited Woman all month and was curious about her. I wanted to get to know her and hear what she had to tell me.

When I got to the woods, I didn't see her at first. She wasn't sitting where we'd first met. Looking around and walking further into the woods, I saw her sitting with her back against a large, old oak. Her long, salt-and-pepper hair, which she wore in one, single braid, rested against the tree. When she saw me, she smiled, said nothing, and patted the spot next to her. I sat down beside her, and rested my back against the tree.

Tree Spirited Woman didn't say anything, and I had a hard time sitting quietly, so I started talking—rambling, actually. She looked at me and smiled.

"Silence is hard for many," she said. I felt a little foolish. She continued, *"When one talks, much is missed. Before we begin, let us sit here and just listen to what is going on around us."*

It was hard, at first, not talking or fidgeting, but I decided to try what she had suggested. I closed my eyes, and started to listen, really listen. I listened first to my own breathing, and then to the sounds all around me. I could hear squirrels scurrying, birds calling to each other, and even insects walking on the dead leaves. This listening brought back the memory of the game Grandmother had played with me when I was young.

As I opened my eyes, a doe was walking slowly behind the trees. I was in awe. I loved the woods, and walked them often. But thinking about it, I never took the time to really see or listen to what was going on around me. My mind was always thinking about something, and I loved to sing or hum while I walked.

When Tree Spirited Woman started to talk, it startled me. *"There is much one misses if time is not taken to hear and see one's surroundings. It pleases me to have shared this quiet time with you. We have much to cover, and time is not long; we must begin."*

"Begin what?" I asked.

She looked at me, smiled, and said, *"Be patient, the answers will come."*

My mind began to race ahead with questions, but suddenly her words interrupted my thoughts. *"Women have questions on many topics. This day, we will focus on the listening."*

I took out the paper and pencil I had brought to take notes. I wanted to make sure I was getting her message down correctly. Tree Spirited Woman looked at me and said, *"Put the paper away. It is not needed. When the time comes, you will write what is to be shared."*

"What if I forget what you say?" I protested. "I need the paper and pencil to take notes, so I get it right."

"Paper and pencil are not necessary. When it is time, what is remembered will be what is written. It

is now time for you to listen, and to hear what will be shared." Then she began.

"There are many gifts one may receive, but none so great as the gift of being heard."

"What do you mean?" I asked.

She gazed into my eyes, then spoke to me as if I were a small child. "It is important for you to sit quietly, so you will understand the meaning of what is being spoken."

She closed her eyes and continued. "One does not communicate with words only. One also communicates with tone of voice and the physical actions of the body. When one truly listens, one sees, one hears, and one feels all that is being spoken.

"Those who truly listen are not thinking of the words that they will soon speak; they are looking at the person who is talking, and understanding all that is being communicated. This gift of listening will leave the person who has been talking with a feeling of having been heard. Too often, people do not listen to others. A question is asked, but the time is not taken to hear the full answer. That often leaves one feeling that she is all alone with her thoughts and emotions.

"If one feels alone for a time, and does not share what is in one's heart and mind, she may become confused or unstable. All people need someone to listen. It is important to the speaker that what has been said, has been heard and understood.

"The gift of listening does not cost money, but it will be greatly treasured by all who receive it."

Tree Spirited Woman looked at me as if she were looking into my very soul and said, "In the next months, you will practice quieting yourself and giving the gift of listening to everyone around you. You will also think of questions to ask that I may answer." She looked away, coughed into her hand, and started to get up.

"It is time for me to leave," she told me.

I was surprised our time was over, but I made no comment. I stood next to her, and we said our good-byes. As she walked away, I closed my eyes. I could hear the leaves crunching under her feet, and I listened until only the sounds of the woods remained.

October 28

I met with Tree Spirited woman today. It was surprisingly fun. She talked about listening being a gift, and then we practiced right there in the woods. I never realized how hard it could be to sit still and really listen. I wanted to take notes and she told me I didn't need to. She said when the time is right, it would come to me. But I know better. So I'm going to try to write down the important things she says. Oh...I hear the kids. More later!

November 10

I thought I would be able to write something every day. Boy, was I wrong! well, at least I'm writing a little something most days. I've been practicing quieting myself. At first it was hard just sitting, listening to my breathing and trying not to let my mind wander. My mind kept going

off in different directions. But it's become
easier. I can actually sit quietly. what's
more, I've gotten comfortable with the
silence. I'm feeling proud of myself. I
might mention this to Tree Spirited woman
when we meet, but I'm not sure.

FOUR

Prayer

The college was about 12 miles from my house and, as I was driving, I was thinking of questions to ask Tree Spirited Woman. For today's meeting, I decided to focus on a question that I'd been thinking about since our first encounter.

The day was cold and breezy. Getting out of my car, I grabbed my jacket and gloves. As I reached the path, I saw Tree Spirited Woman waiting for me, and I ran to join her. After saying hello, we walked in silence, and I hoped she'd noticed I wasn't rambling. We came upon an old log resting across the path when she said, *"This spot is perfect."*

Sitting next to her on the log, I waited for an opportunity to ask my question. Taking a deep breath, I began. "When you told me how you were given the name 'Tree Spirited Woman', you said you were praying as you had never prayed before. I've tried to pray, but I get confused. Can you explain prayer to me?"

She looked at me and said nothing. Closing her eyes, she quieted herself before answering. *"Prayer is something one does,"* she said softly.

"I understand that. But, can you explain prayer's importance, and is there a right or wrong way to pray?" I persisted.

"I will tell it best, if I tell you why I pray," she replied.

"That's perfect," I told her. "You can explain prayer any way you want. I just need to understand prayer's importance, so I'll know what to write."

As she closed her eyes, she seemed to be visualizing her words. Quietly she said, *"I will begin now.*

"I pray to a God, who is always with me. It is often in prayer that I am most thankful. Life has not always been easy, yet life has always been good. The hardest of life's lessons have given me much for which to be thankful. These lessons have molded me into

who I am on this day. When I pray, I am always thankful for all I have been given, and it is in prayer that I seek the guidance to do what I must do."

Tree Spirited Woman opened her eyes for a brief moment, then looked directly into mine and said, *"It is important to tell others that praying is the way one talks with God about one's life."* She then closed her eyes and continued. *"God hears prayers. It is important that one listens for an answer, or one may not hear. Answers to prayers may not be what one wants or expects. Still, prayers are heard, and whatever God's answer, it is best for the life journey.*

"When one prays, she is able to release something from within and share it with another. Sometimes prayer is also used as a cry for help, sometimes to beg for forgiveness, sometimes to rejoice. Prayer is a reminder that one is never alone.

"Prayers can be long, or prayers can be short. Prayers can be said aloud or reflected silently, on one's knees or while walking. It does not matter how or where one prays. What is important is that the prayer comes from the heart. God hears all prayers." She opened her eyes, smiled, and said, *"That is why I pray."*

"That was beautiful," I replied. "You must have a lot of faith. Are you a spiritual person?" I asked.

"*I believe,*" she said with a twinkle in her eye. "*Are you now asking me what is faith?*"

"I guess I am," I said laughing.

When Tree Spirited Woman smiled at me, her face became alive with a radiant glow. Staring at her, I felt her peace envelop my soul. She continued.

"*Faith is believing in what one cannot see. My faith is knowing that God is leading me in life, and I must listen in order to hear what God wishes me to do. Everyone is meant to have a life journey. Faith is believing in that journey.*"

"Is talking to you part of my journey?" I questioned.

"*I believe that to be true,*" she replied. "*It is time for you to look into your soul, and pray to find your answers.*"

I closed my eyes, and talked with God for a very long while. Tears flowed down my cheeks, and I could feel changes happening within me. At that moment, I knew I would never again be alone. God would be my guide.

When I opened my eyes, I was surprised to see that Tree Spirited Woman had gone. Getting up to leave, I smiled to myself and felt excited about my life.

December 12

I've been praying daily since my meeting with Tree Spirited Woman. During my quiet time seems to work best. I have also been thinking a lot about Grandmother. Her presence is constantly with me. I miss her so much. I wish she were here so I could tell her all about Tree Spirited Woman. But I believe she knows all about her. They are so much alike; it's spooky and comforting at the same time.

December 23

It's difficult knowing what to write in this journal. I try to quiet myself, yet my mind seems to be in constant motion. Will I ever totally learn to quiet my thoughts? Do I even want to? I've been meeting with Tree Spirited Woman for a few months, and I still don't understand why she thinks I'll be able to write her stories.

PRAYER

OK, God—if writing is something I'm suppose to eventually do, I really need your help. So please guide me.

FIVE

Truth

On the 28th of December it snowed about 6 inches. As I was putting on my long underwear, I began to question whether Tree Spirited Woman would show up for our meeting. I considered skipping our standing appointment. I didn't want to go wandering in the woods on a day like this; it was cold and wet. Still, I knew if I didn't go and she showed up, I'd feel like I'd let her down.

Trudging through the woods, dressed in double layers, I started to get warm. I'd been walking about a mile and still saw no sign of Tree Spirited Woman. I decided I'd walk another ten minutes before starting back to my car. I was just ready to turn back when I spotted her. She had spread out a blue plastic tarp, the kind you might put under a tent, and she was sitting on it, sipping something steaming from a large cup. A thermos, along with an extra cup, was on the tarp beside her.

She looked up and said, *"It is good to see you. Come and have a cup of cider with me as we talk."* As I sat down next to her, I filled my cup, and she continued, *"You have the look of someone who has a question to ask."* Tree Spirited Woman smiled at me and waited for me to begin.

"I have had many people tell me things they say are true, yet, when I talk to someone else, I hear a different story. Can you tell me how I will know who is telling the truth?" I asked.

Tree Spirited Woman looked at me with a sparkle in her eye and started to laugh. *"What you have said is true. People see situations differently and often argue about what is true. What people do not understand is that what they see or believe is their truth. I would like you to stand next to the birch tree near that large elm."*

I slowly stood and walked to where she pointed. I couldn't see Tree Spirited Woman from where I was; the tree was blocking her.

"Now, look closely at the tree and tell me exactly what you see," she directed.

"Well, there is a small patch on the birch tree that looks like someone has written on it. There is also a dead branch hanging down, resting against the trunk of the tree, and it looks like the deer may have eaten away some of its bark."

Looking at the tree, she said to me, *"That is not my tree you are describing, for there is nothing that looks like writing anywhere on my tree, and it has no dead branches hanging down."*

"Wait a minute. Are you describing the birch tree here?" I said, moving where she could see me and pointing to the tree.

"Yes, that is the one I see, and that is the one I am describing."

"There is writing or something that looks like writing on it, and a dead branch is hanging down along the side," I insisted.

"You are mistaken," she told me.

I started to get angry. I knew what I was saying was true. That's when she looked at me with that twinkle in her eye and asked me to come and stand next to her.

When I was by her side, she began, *"Look at my tree, and tell me what you see."* I looked closely at the tree. There was nothing that looked like writing or a dead branch anywhere.

"You're right." I said, "From here, I don't see the writing or the dead branch."

"It is important to listen to others, and to accept that there may be many truths to one story." Tree Spirited Woman then continued, *"When people disagree, they fail to understand that both can be right. For every truth, there is an opposite truth. That is the way it is in life."*

"Well, what of the people who intentionally tell lies?" I asked.

"There will be some who intentionally hide the truth. These people are often afraid of what the truth may bring, or they may have the need to impress others by their stories. Unfortunately, these people have yet to learn that not being truthful makes many of their life problems." Looking into my eyes, she continued, *"Do not judge these people harshly. It is not one's place to cast judgment among others."*

Just then a deer ran through the woods, startling me. Tree Spirited Woman slowly stood, looked at me, and said, *"It is my sign. The cider is gone, and I am cold."* She waited for me to get up.

As I stepped off the tarp, I sensed her age and fragility.

"Do you need any help?" I asked.

Shaking her head, she smiled and said, *"I have enjoyed this visit. I will see you next month."* Then I watched as she leisurely stuffed the tarp in her bag, and walked away through the snowy, silent woods.

January 4

I had an interesting meeting with Tree Spirited Woman last week. We talked about truth. I never really thought about how there could be more than one truth for the same thing. She said for each truth there can be an opposite truth. I've been doing a lot of thinking about that. Just today, my sister told me about a situation, and for the first time I could totally understand that for her it was true. I didn't have to agree with her, and it was ok. I guess that also goes for those who have a different worldview than mine. Their belief is as true to them as mine is to me. Interesting.

January 23

I have been running all day and still haven't completed everything on my list. I could accomplish much more if other people would just do what they said they were going to do. I get so frustrated with some people that my mouth seems to take on a mind of its own. Oh well, I won't have to face them for a while.

SIX

Relationships

Another month had passed, and the day looked magical. The air was crisp, and a heavy frost hung on the trees, causing everything to look like a winter wonderland. I couldn't wait to get into the woods to be a part of the beauty.

I had been thinking about relationships and how, in different settings, they vary so. Deep in thought, I headed down the path, wondering where I would find Tree Spirited Woman today. When I looked up, I saw her waiting for me. I waved, put on my hat and gloves, and then ran to catch up to her. I followed her down the frozen trail, all the while enjoying the cool breeze blowing against my cheeks and being mesmerized by the beauty that surrounded me. I just kept smiling to myself and thinking how much I loved it out here. We walked for about half an hour when Tree Spirited Woman strayed from the path into a clearing. She looked around, laid down her tarp, and then slowly sat. I joined her. We sat without talking for about ten minutes, just enjoying the sounds, the smells, and the beauty that was all around us. Breaking the silence, I told Tree Spirited Woman I had been thinking about relationships and would like to know her view on the subject.

Smiling, Tree Spirited Woman began, "*There are many different relationships one will have in a lifetime. One may have relationships with parents, friends, strangers, lovers, children, and grandchildren. It is important to know each relationship is meant to be.*"

"Even with strangers?" I interrupted.

"*It is often with strangers that we learn the most of who we are. How one treats a stranger tells much about oneself. Are you kind to the salesperson or to the poor who live on the street? One's actions speak loudly.*"

"Are you saying that I'm to be nice to the people who call me at home during supper trying to sell me things?"

"One can be respectful, and still say no." She looked up at me, smiled, and went on, *"Each friend…"*

"Wait, I have a question," I said, interrupting her. "How is it that I can have so many different kinds of relationships. I mean, some are intellectual, some spiritual, and some nonspirtual. In some relationships, I can laugh and be silly, and others know me only by my serious side. Sometimes it feels like no one knows the real me." Then I laughed and said, "Heck, sometimes, I don't even know myself."

Smiling, Tree Spirited Woman continued, *"One relationship cannot fulfill every need in one's life. In a lifetime, there will be many encounters with others, some will be brief, and others will form into longer relationships.*

"Each person is put into one's life for a purpose. We are to learn from one another. Every person has needs, and those needs are met by the many different relationships one has. A person may be put in

your life not because of the need **you** *have or the lesson* **you** *are to learn, but for the need or the lesson* **they** *are to learn. One must be open to all who come in contact with them; whether they are friends, strangers, acquaintances, or family. Each friend was once a stranger. Every relationship is a gift. How one treats others will affect every area of one's life."*

My thoughts started to race. I remembered how rude I had been to the lady at the store earlier that day. Was that how I wanted her to remember me? Did my actions and words affect the rest of her day? I could no longer concentrate on what Tree Spirited Woman was saying. My mind was playing back the words and the attitude I had used in that morning's encounter.

Tree Spirited Woman sensed my anxiety and quietly told me, *"It is right for you to leave."*

Saying nothing, I got up and walked toward the path. I knew I had to see if the woman was still at work. I felt the need to apologize for my rudeness.

Just that morning I had stopped at the grocery store. The people around me were slow and, as usual, I was in a hurry. I waited in the checkout line for ten minutes. When it was my turn, the lady said, "I need to close for my break." I was so angry,

I said things I don't want to repeat. She got mad and went to get the manager to wait on me. I'm sure if I had just explained in a friendlier tone how long I had been waiting, she would have reacted differently. I didn't want her to remember me as the witch who went through her line.

I was disappointed to find that the woman wasn't working at the store when I stopped on my way home. Undeterred in my effort to make amends, however, I stopped in again the next morning. I waited in her line, and when it was my turn I said, "I was here yesterday, and I was very rude to you. I want to apologize."

She looked shocked. Then she said, "Oh, its ok; everyone has a bad day."

"Yes, they do, but it still wasn't right for me to take it out on you. I'm sorry." I smiled and said, "I hope you have a good day." Then I left. I don't know if my apology made any difference in her day, but it sure did in mine!

February 1

I stopped in at the store today and told the cashier I was sorry I was so rude yesterday. I felt awful and she tried to make me feel better by saying everyone has a bad day now and then. I sure can get crabby at times, and I hate it when I speak before I think. Why can't I remember that some things are just better not said!

February 9

Tree Spirited Woman's words on listening and learning from relationships have caused me to be more aware of my tone and actions. I have been trying to be careful with how I communicate with others and, at times, it's been very difficult. I guess no one ever said it was going to be easy.

God, I'm here again, and I really need your help making me aware of how I'm communicating.

SEVEN

Marriage

The days were warming; the snow was slowly melting. Today was cloudy and misting lightly. I had on my fleece jacket and, as I got out of the car, I grabbed my rain poncho, hoping I'd be warm enough.

Tree Spirited Woman was waiting for me near the entrance of the woods. I was surprised; usually I had to walk some distance before seeing her.

As we walked together down the path, Tree Spirited Woman hummed a soft melody. She led me onto a little trail that brought us to a small, egg-shaped pond. There was still 2 to 3 inches of ice on the pond, and a number of dead trees were standing near the edge, partially submerged. We found a small clearing near the water's edge, and Tree Spirited Woman put down her blue tarp. I was thankful she'd brought it.

Tree Spirited Woman smiled at me and said softly, *"Today I will talk about marriage. I have reflected much, and now I will share what I know."*

Her choice of topic intrigued me. I had been feeling guilt about my divorce recently, and just this week I had wondered if I would ever try marriage again.

Her voice interrupted my thoughts. *"Marriage is when two people choose to love one another and commit to a lifelong relationship. When two agree to marry, it is meant to be for a lifetime. The commitment of marriage means that you will trust your love for the other, even on days when one does not feel the love. It means compromising what one wants for what is best for the two. It means sharing one's time, money, and energy. It is sharing in one another's sorrow, illness, and happiness. Marriage does not put restrictions on one another. Instead, marriage encourages each to become the person they are meant to be. It is no longer living for just the 'Me.' It is choosing to live for the 'We'. It is in giving a part of oneself each day that one makes a marriage last for a lifetime.*

"There are some things that are a mystery, such as how two can become one. Water cannot be separated into parts and still be water; so it is with the partners in a loving marriage."

"That's it? That's what makes a successful marriage?" I asked.

She looked at me patiently, shook her head, smiled her half smile, and continued, "Prayer is also important for a marriage. The two must pray together each day, asking God to continually make the marriage grow stronger. This prayer will be a constant reminder of the commitment the two have made to one another."

"Is marriage for everyone?" I questioned.

"Marriage is a choice, a choice not everyone needs to make. If two choose to be married, then this choice can be the soil from where the marriage will grow."

I was listening to everything she was saying, and I realized that I'd never been in a committed marriage.

Interrupting my thoughts, she continued, "Not all are to be married, and not all marriages will succeed." I looked at her waiting for her to continue.

"That does not mean we are meant to be alone. There are many ways to share one's life with others.

One may be through a loving partnership; others may happen in the workplace, where one worships, or in one's community.

"In every relationship, each person comes with different histories and beliefs. They try to put everything together in a way that works for all. This is not easy. Committed relationships take work, and are successful when filled with love, patience, and respect.

"It is not for me to say marriage is for everyone. It is not. When two commit to working on their marriage, the marriage will be for their lifetime." Tree Spirited Woman gazed into my eyes, and I felt she wanted to reach into my heart. Then she smiled and said softly, "*Good marriages do happen.*"

Closing her eyes, Tree Spirited Woman sat quietly for a few minutes. My mind turned over everything she had shared, and for the first time, I thought I would like to experience a good marriage.

It was getting late, and I needed to leave for a date I'd made for dinner. As I stood, I asked if she wanted any help putting the tarp away. Smiling up at me, she shook her head. I said good-bye. She was still smiling up at me when she said, "*Have an enjoyable dinner.*"

Walking back to my car, I realized I hadn't mentioned anything about my dinner date. How did she always seem to know?

March 2

I have talked to Jim every night since our dinner date. It has been so much fun talking and laughing with someone. I really enjoy his company, but I don't think I'm ready for a long-term relationship. I still have junk I have to deal with—my ex, and how to balance my time. Will a relationship ever be right for me?

March 27

I meet with Tree Spirited Woman tomorrow and as I reflect on my last meeting with her, I find myself smiling. A lot has happened to me this past month. My dinner date turned out to be a wonderful month of talking and spending time with someone special. Who knows what the future will hold? For now, I'm enjoying all the attention and the warm feelings. I wonder if Tree Spirited Woman will see a difference.

EIGHT

Children

A light breeze was coming from the south, and the smell of spring was in the air. The sun was shining, and the warmth on my cheeks felt wonderful. Looking around, I noticed small buds starting to form on the trees. New life, new beginnings, I thought as I walked down the path, smiling to myself. I was remembering what Tree Spirited Woman had shared the first time we met, about spring being the time to try new ideas and take risks. I wondered what she would talk about today. Closing my eyes and taking in the scent of fresh pine and the dampness rising from the ground, I raised my arms high into the air and was absorbed by the moment. When I finally opened my eyes, I saw Tree Spirited Woman watching me. Smiling at her, I asked, "Isn't it a beautiful day?"

With that twinkle in her eye she said, *"Yes, this day is special. I will spend it with you. Come, let us find a nice place in which to talk."*

We walked in silence for about ten minutes, enjoying everything around us, when suddenly Tree Spirited Woman coughed long and hard and seemed to lose her breath.

"Are you all right?" I asked.

"I will be fine. Let us sit by this tree so I can rest my back," she said as we walked toward a large, old cottonwood that seemed to be standing alone.

I wanted to ask Tree Spirited Woman how she was feeling, and if everything was okay. She wasn't a large woman, about 5 foot 3, and 130 pounds. She looked pale, and it seemed she had been losing weight. As if reading my mind, Tree Spirited Woman looked at me and said tenderly, *"Everything is as it should be."* I felt worried, but her soft breathing calmed me. Then she began, *"The trees and shrubs are sprouting new life; it is the right time to talk of children.*

"Children are the window to the future and the mirror to the past. A child allows one to see from

where one has come and to dream about where one may go. Sometimes, as we age, it takes a child to help up remember our youth.

"Each child's journey will be unique. As a parent, one can either act as the guide, and be the light that shines forward, or the restraint that holds them firm. Often parents want their own lost dreams for their child. But the wise parent listens and encourages the child. A child's journey is not easy. The child must bravely step into a world where only the child can go, and the parent can only imagine."

"I never thought of a child's life as being a journey," I said. "I sometimes think the children of today are kind of messed up, and I pray each day that my children will grow up with a positive outlook."

"The children of today are really no different than the children of yesterday. Children of the past, as well as children of the present, laugh, cry, and want to be accepted by others. Children are no more, as you say, 'messed up' today than they were in generations past."

Tree Spirited Woman pointed to the little buds on the tree and continued, "See the small buds forming? They are the tree's future. Those buds are the leaves of tomorrow. They will sprout, grow, flow in the wind, shout out with color, let go, and move *on. It is the same with children; the buds will turn into leaves, the children will grow into adults. The children of today will make the choices for the future. The future is always in the hands of the children.*

"Everyone is someone's child. The child always lives within us and, on occasion, it is good to be as a child." She cupped my face in her hands, looked deep in my eyes and slowly said, *"It is important for you to take time to enjoy life as a child. You must be childlike in order to see the goodness and beauty in everyone and everything around you. It is by experiencing the world through the child inside that you fully become the nurturing adult."* She held my face a moment longer, then she let go.

Tree Spirited Woman closed her eyes and sat quietly for a few minutes. As she opened her eyes and looked at me, she smiled, reached out her hands to me, and said, *"Help me up. Let us walk together and enjoy this time."* I took hold of her hands and pulled her to her feet. Together we walked down the trail, taking in all the sounds and smells that surrounded us. Our talking for the day was over.

April 5

   After hearing Tree Spirited Woman talk
about children, I came home and enjoyed
the evening with my son and daughter.
I have always appreciated having my
children, I just didn't realize how much.
I knew I was lucky to have beautiful,
healthy children. My son will be starting
school next fall, and I never planned
on having another child. Yet, throughout
this past week, I've had a reoccurring
dream that I was holding a baby. Could
it be Tree Spirited Woman's words that
sparked these feelings within me, or could
it be the new relationship I'm in? Or could
it just be the new beginnings?

April 20

   I am surprised and please to
recognize how I have changed since
first meeting Tree Spirited Woman. I have
learned to quiet myself, appreciate the

beauty that surrounds me, think before I speak, and I'm falling in love again. who would have thought so much could happen in just a few short months. I wonder what other experiences are in store for me during this life journey!

April 27

Tree Spirited Woman isn't well, and that saddens me. Our monthly meetings rarely go over an hour. Yet, could they be a strain on her health? I hope she gets better; we still have many topics to discuss.

NINE

Menopause

My body was in its childbearing years; yet, I had questions about what would happen to my body as it aged. I decided today to ask Tree Spirited Woman about menopause. Menopause seemed to be a big subject lately. All the magazines contained something on it, and someday I would experience it. As I thought about my meeting with Tree Spirited Woman, I wondered what she'd have to say about the subject.

"Good afternoon," I yelled, seeing Tree Spirited Woman sitting on a dead tree that had fallen across the flowing stream. Her pant legs were rolled up; she was barefoot, and her feet were dangling in the water. She looked up, smiled, and waved. I started to jog up the deer path, and was out of breath by the time I reached her.

She looked up at me in the way one might look at a small child, then patiently said, *"Life passes too quickly to always be in a hurry."* Without another word, she moved over to make room for me. I took off my shoes and put my feet next to hers. The water was very cold but refreshing.

"Do you have something you would like to talk about today?" I asked.

"No. This day, we will talk on what you choose," she replied with that twinkle in her eye.

I felt she knew I had already decided on a topic. Grinning, I slowly said, "Men-o-pause." She just chuckled, closed her eyes, sat quietly for a few moments, and then spoke.

"Menopause is a gift a woman receives when her body tells her it is time for change. Menopause happens to both the male and female. It is funny to me that men often think menopause is only for the women. The word 'men-o-pause' includes 'men' and 'pause'. It is a time for both male and female to slow their pace."

Looking at me, she asked, *"With the word 'men' in menopause, why do men not see that they, too, are* to be included in this physical journey?" I shrugged my shoulders, and she continued.

"*Menopause is a natural progression in one's life. It is the time when one must let go of their past in order to move to their future. For some, menopause can be a time of remorse, a time when one feels old and no longer productive. For others, it can be a time of personal reflection with anticipation for the future. When two people care for one another and they reach this stage together, it can be a time of conflict, or a time of growth. It is for each individual to decide how they will travel through this chapter in their life.*"

"Just a minute," I interrupted. "I want to know, why do so many people struggle during menopause, and how can I get through it without any problems."

She chuckled, "*First, people who struggle through menopause, often struggle with many areas in their lives. They have grown accustomed to the feelings of discontentment and are in the habit of making complaints. They know no other way. When one is used to a feeling or an action, it is uncomfortable to feel or act differently. But it is not impossible. One's feelings and actions can become a habit, and habits can be difficult to break. But, with work, it can be done.*

"Sometimes there can be physical difficulties in one's life. Some difficulties can be controlled if one eats properly, gets exercise, uses herbs, or follows Eastern or Western medicines. Other physical ailments may need more treatments.

"You asked how you could experience menopause without problems. It is important to listen to your body and to take care of it. Your body houses your soul, your spirit, your life force. You only get one body; it is important to listen to what it says, and to respect it.

"It is not uncommon to fear the unknown, and menopause is an unknown. Each person will go through menopause differently. I cannot say what will make your physical journey easier. Only you can do that. You can make it easier if you believe it will be one of ease. How one perceives the journey is of most importance.

"Menopause is a time in one's life, much like the adolescent years, time when one can take new risks, reach out to others, and celebrate the new person she is to become. This can be an exciting or a depressing time in one's life. Again, much will depend on how one perceives the journey."

"Wait! Are you saying…?" I started to ask.

She held up her hand to silence me and said, *"You have heard the words. When it is your time to experience menopause, it will be another journey for you to take. No two paths are exactly the same."*

As Tree Spirited Woman reached for her shoes, she said, *"It is time for me to leave."*

I realized I didn't want our time to end. "Couldn't we just sit here awhile longer?" I asked.

Tree Spirited Woman looked at me with a tired smile and said, *"Another time. For now, I must go."* She put on her shoes, slowly stood up, and shuffled down the deer path.

As I watched her go, I knew these times together were a special gift. Although I still wondered why she had chosen me, I was honored to be the keeper of her wisdom.

May 5

Some days it's extremely hard being a single mom. Today was tough. The kids were arguing and I was running out of patience. This was to be my weekend without kids, and I was looking forward to my time alone. My Ex came to pick up the kids three hours late. I tried to make light of it and not say anything negative. When they finally left, I had a good cry, filled the bathtub, lit candles, and soaked until I was wrinkled. Now I feel much better!

May 11

It's hard to believe that nine months have passed since my first meeting with Tree Spirited Woman. Here I am, continuing to go month after month, looking forward to the 28th.. The date is marked on my calendar, and I have rearranged my activities, so I'll always be free on that day. I can't believe how my skepticism has turned to anticipation of our monthly meeting. I do wonder where she goes when she leaves me. Maybe one of these months I'll ask her.

TEN

Age

I started into the woods, looked around at the trees and foliage, and was impressed with all the variations of green. The weather felt like mid-summer, and the summer solstice was still about a month away. As I walked, enjoying the smells and the warm air, I saw Tree Spirited Woman on the path ahead, waiting for me.

When I reached her, she smiled, took my arm, and led me to a grassy spot where she had already placed an old blanket. *"I am so pleased you are here,"* she said as we sat down. For a moment, I wondered if she actually thought I wouldn't come. *"Before we begin, you must connect with this spot,"* she said smiling.

I knew this was her way of quieting me down. Being a Type A personality, this quieting down time had become a helpful technique that I now used in my everyday life. Closing my eyes, I took some deep breaths, and listened to all the sounds surrounding me. Lost in my own quieting moment, I heard her say, *"I am tired. My time is near."*

Looking at Tree Spirited Woman I said, "You've told me before that you're tired and your time is growing near. I'm not sure what you mean. It worries me. Are you sick? How old are you, anyway?"

Tree Spirited Woman looked further into the woods, and for a moment seemed to be drifting into a trance. Then she began, *"Age is but a number one uses to recognize the years that have past. If someone is in the upper numbers, society considers them old."* She then looked at me and continued, *"You can be as old or as young as your body or mind will let you be. When one has lived many years, the body is not always able to do what it once could as a child. The body has many ways of letting us know what it needs. As the body tires, it lets one know it is time to take life at a slower pace."*

"Does that mean if I want to stay young, I will?" I asked.

She smiled at me and patiently continued her explanation. *"One will age through life's experiences and years. The body will change and the face will line; that is true. Do these changes mean one is old, or that one has lived many years?"* she asked me.

"Aren't they one and the same?" I answered.

She laughed, *"Have you not seen someone who has lined long before someone else who has lived as long? Does that mean one is old and one is young?"* she asked.

"Well, I don't know." I replied.

"It is true we all will age and grow older. Living as if one was old comes from one's belief. If one can be active with one's body, it will not age as quickly. As one ages, walking does not need to be as quick as when one was a youth. The body reminds one they no longer have to be in a hurry. Time passes swiftly enough," she said.

Tree Spirited Woman continued, *"If one stays healthy, and the memory strong, it is important that one continues to learn and grow. The mind is always open to new ideas and thoughts. That does not stop when one has lived many years.*

"There will be some who will be old because they believe what others tell them. Their age number

is high, and they are told they are old; so they will become so. Others will not listen to the words, and will continue to live life to the fullest. They will slow, but they will not hear when others tell them they cannot do something because of their age. Those who do not listen will live a fuller life.

"I am one who has lived a full life. I quit counting years and have lived each day of my life. Many of my days have been filled with happiness, and many of the days filled with sorrow. I am pleased I have had many life experiences and would choose to give up none, for I have become the person I am because of all those life experiences and lessons."

She looked me in the eye and said, "That is how I feel about age. It is for you to decide how you will let others influence your beliefs and how you will choose to live your years."

Quietly sitting next to Tree Spirited Woman thinking about everything she had just shared, I remembered I had made a date with Jim. I stood saying, "I'm sorry, I have to get going. I have something planned for later this afternoon."

Heading toward the parking lot, I thought more about aging. I knew people who were old far before their time and others who were still living their lives to the fullest. Tree Spirited Woman was right; society did judge people by their age number. I decided then that I would live my life to the fullest and find some pleasure in each day. Getting into my car, I turned the radio up loud and started singing along.

May 30

I only just realized that Tree Spirited woman never answered my question when I asked her if she was sick. I wonder if it was intentional.

June 5

Dad just had his birthday and we all got together. I looked at him and thought his number is getting high, yet he lives life to the fullest, and no one would ever guess his age. Why does everyone put such an importance on the number? I've decided to be like Dad and stay active and enjoy every day.

June 25

My good friend, Jen, was just diagnosed with uterine cancer and she goes in for exploratory surgery tomorrow. I pray everything will be fine. The doctors aren't sure how bad it is. They won't know until they open her up.

Dear God, please be with Jen and her family and help them through this.

ELEVEN

Death

How fast a month goes by, I thought, dragging myself out of bed. The day looked the way I felt, gray, no sunshine anywhere, and a light rain was falling. My mind was roaming; I wanted to turn it off. I didn't want to think. It was late and it was almost time for my meeting with Tree Spirited Woman. Putting off the start of the day as long as I could, I dressed.

As I reached the empty parking lot, I decided to leave my car right in the middle, all alone. Grabbing my rain jacket, I walked down the path. I had walked further than usual before spotting her. Even though the air was warm, Tree Spirited Woman had an old blanket wrapped around her shoulders, protecting her from the rain. She was sitting on a tree that the wind had blown over. As I got closer, she turned and looked at me. Her expression was serious. She patted the spot next to her and I sat down, saying nothing. I really didn't feel like being here. "*You have much on your mind,*" she said to me and waited for me to begin.

"I have a good friend who was just diagnosed with uterine cancer. A couple of days ago they were going to do some exploratory surgery. When the doctors opened her up, the cancer had spread. They had to perform a complete hysterectomy. The doctors told her they would now have to wait and see." The tears started to come. "Life just isn't fair! She's only been married a few years. They were trying to start a family. Now…," I couldn't go on. I started to sob.

The sobs seemed to come from somewhere deep within myself. Tree Spirited Woman sat, letting me cry. When I was cried out, she looked at me and asked, "*Would you like to talk about death?*" Saying nothing, I nodded.

"*Life is a cycle. It begins and it ends. In the middle is what we call living. How we live life is different for each. No one knows if her life cycle will be long or if it will be short.*

"Everything has a life cycle. Each day, each month, and each year has a beginning and an ending. All that lives, dies: the butterfly, the deer, the flower, the tree, and the human. It is only the human that worries about death.

"When someone dies, they are physically gone. Still, a part of them lives on through all the lives they have touched. As with your friend, when it is her time, her physical body will die, yet her spirit will live on through all those who keep her alive in their memory. Life is like the river, it constantly moves, but it is always here."

"But why is death so hard for the living!" I shouted.

"One does not want things to change, and death is change," she told me patiently. *"Death is often easier to accept for the one who is dying than for those it leaves behind. Death is a time to celebrate one's life: a time to remember through tears, laughter, and stories. Death is not to be thought of as a punishment, it will happen to all things that live. When you think of your friend, cherish her life and the time you spend with her."*

"Are you dying?" I asked.

"We are all dying," she replied.

"That's not what I meant and you know it!" I yelled.

She looked at me and her eyes seemed to penetrate to my soul. *"It is true, my time is getting short."*

My eyes filled with tears as she took my hands into hers. I could feel her warmth as she held on to them, stroking each hand gently. *"I will not be lost to you. The words I have spoken will be with you always. As you share them with others, a part of me continues to live. Life has been a gift, and I have lived it well. When it is time for me to no longer live in this world, I will pass on. It is part of the cycle. I have had my beginning and when it is time, I will reach my end."*

I was crying again. Tree Spirited Woman still held my hands. *"It is good to cry. Crying cleanses the soul. When one feels sadness, it is not for those who have died, it is sadness for all the losses in one's life. Every time someone dies, the future has been changed."*

As I looked at her, she continued, *"When we can no longer meet, it will be time for you to put my words into a book that will be shared with others. It will be through this book that you can change your life and the lives of others."*

I had nothing more to say. We sat quietly enjoying each other's company. It was enough. A storm was threatening, and it was getting dark. Feeling like I had been drained of all emotion, I asked weakly, "Will I see you again?"

"I will come as long as I am able," she answered.

I stood and pulled her up to stand beside me. Tree Spirited Woman locked her arm in mine, and we slowly walked back to the parking lot. As she left me, the tears started to flow down my cheeks. It was at that moment I realized I was crying for my friend and for the time I would no longer be meeting with Tree Spirited Women.

July 3

I've been over to see Jen, and her spirits are high. I'm looking forward to telling Tree Spirited Women about Jen. Because of the kind of cancer she has, the doctors are optimistic. Miracles do happen, and my friend and her husband have a lot of faith. They are already discussing adoption. It won't be for some time, but it's a good sign.

Dear God, I just want to Thank you for being with Jen and her family. Thank you for listening.

July 12

My relationship with Jim is wonderful! He treats me special. But I don't feel worthy of his love, or is it that I don't trust it? I have so much junk from my ex that I'm trying to work out. I still can hear him yelling, then I relive the feeling that everything was my fault. I'm so confused. What is wrong with me that I can't seem to move on?

July 26

Last month I was so concerned with Jen that I forgot to ask Tree Spirited Woman if she was sick. This month I'll ask her about her health.

TWELVE

Trust

The day was hot, humid, and the air was sticky. Grabbing my water bottle, I started down the path that had become so familiar to me. I looked around trying to spot Tree Spirited Woman. She was never in the same area twice. Gazing uphill to the right of the path, I saw her standing, and she appeared to be staring at something in the distance. Her back was toward me; she looked small and frail. I yelled her name; she turned and motioned for me to come join her. Running up the hill, I could feel my body relax. I realized it was the feeling I always got whenever I came to these woods for my meetings with Tree Spirited Woman.

When I reached Tree Spirited Woman, she smiled, hooked her arm in mine, and we continued slowly down the path. We'd been walking, arm-in-arm, in silence for about fifteen minutes, when a hawk landed ahead of us. We stopped and watched. The hawk stood on the side of the path, and seemed to be looking directly at me. Then the hawk flew up, circled us twice, and flew away.

Before I could say anything, Tree Spirited Woman said, *"Come, let us sit together. I have something you must hear."* She led me toward a downed tree, where we sat next to each other.

Tree Spirited Woman looked at me and said, *"You have a strong animal sign. That hawk was sent to give you important medicine."*

"Medicine? I don't understand," I said.

"Animals often carry important medicine to those who listen."

Taking my hands in hers, and looking into my eyes, Tree Spirited Woman said, *"This medicine brings personal power, strength, and understanding. It is the constant living of life that brings healing to the body, mind, and spirit."* Tree Spirited Woman looked up at the sky, closed her eyes, and continued, *"You must think of the hawk that is hungry. The hawk swoops down to catch its food and if the prey is too large to carry, the hawk must let go and trust it will find other food. If the hawk does not let go and trust, and continues to hold on, it will die of starvation.*" Tree Spirited Woman looked at me intensely and continued, "*The hawk was telling you to let go and trust. All will be as God intends. What one might wish to happen is not always meant to be.*"

The look on my face must have been one of surprise. I had been seeing a number of hawks lately, which I'd thought strange. Interrupting my thoughts, Tree Spirited Woman said, "*Often, one holds on to the pain of the past, or worries about a situation one cannot control. If one does not learn to 'Let go and Trust,' one's body, mind, or spirit can be destroyed.*"

Tree Spirited Woman started to cough long and hard. She took out a tissue, and wiped her mouth. That's when I saw specks of blood. "Are you all right?" I asked.

Tree Spirit Woman smiled and started to stand. "*Walk with me for awhile,*" she said. Hooking my arm in hers, we started back the way we had come.

"You're sick, aren't you?" I asked.

Tree Spirited Woman did not reply right away. Then she said quietly, "*It is true. I am not well.*"

I started to ask more questions, when she held up her hand to quiet me.

"Let us talk more at our next meeting." I started to protest, when a hawk flew by, startling me. Smiling, Tree Spirited Woman said, *"Let go and trust."*

I started to ask a question, when Tree Spirited Woman said, *"It is time for you to leave. I will be staying awhile longer."* Unhooking her arm from mine, she gave me a gentle push.

It was obvious, Tree Spirited Woman didn't want to talk anymore. I reluctantly said good-bye, and walked slowly back to my car.

July 30

Tree Spirited Woman isn't well and I can't get her to talk about it.

I worry about her. I've been thinking about what she said about the hawk, and I remember a hawk being in my dreams about Grandmother.

Grandmother, were you trying to tell me that I needed to let go and trust? It sounds so easy, yet I know it's so difficult.

God, I'm sending another postcard prayer your way. I really need your help, letting go and trusting. It's out of my hands. I'm turning it all over to you.

August 18

I feel blessed to have had the opportunity to meet with Tree Spirited woman over these last few months. And to think I almost didn't go. I'm trying to write down things she shares with me each month. Hope I'm doing a good enough job with it. I guess only time will tell.

THIRTEEN

Joy

After our last meeting, it was obvious to me that Tree Spirited Woman was more ill than I had wanted to believe. I was worried about her health, and didn't know if she would seek the medical attention she needed, or if she'd just let life run its course. I decided to confront her with my concerns about her health.

Parking my car, I noticed that there wasn't anyone else there. That's the way it had been almost every month. I was saddened that nobody else seemed to take advantage of these woods. What a waste. This was one of the most beautiful spots in the area, and no one was ever here.

Leaving the parking lot, I started down the trail. I hadn't gone very far when I saw Tree Spirited Woman sitting on her blanket. She looked deep in thought, and not wanting to startle her, I softly called her name. It took a moment before she looked up. Her smile was inviting, and I walked over to join her. As I sat down, she said, *"What a joy it has been for me to know you."* Smiling at her, I told her I had also enjoyed our time together.

Tree Spirited Woman looked tired, but continued, *"Today, I wish to talk of being joyful and having joy in one's heart. If one is joyful, she will have peace within. Joy is what some may call happiness, bliss, tranquility, or a variety of other names. No matter, I call it joy.*

"Joy is in everything. When one is open to life, joy will find them. Joy is a child smiling, a flower blooming, squirrels playing, a walk in the woods, or sitting on the beach. Joy is living in the moment."

"I know people who always focus on the negative and don't seem happy. Can they become joyful?" I asked.

"Joy is within everyone; whether to be happy or sad is of one's own choosing. One's thought process can become a habit. When one becomes comfortable with complaining or having stress in one's life, it is dif-

ficult to change. Negative thoughts spread like raging fire, but fire can be stopped. One always has a choice as to how one will view life. It is up to each to decide to experience or not to experience joy in one's life.

"There are some who believe if they do not feel happiness, they do not have joy within. That is not true. Still, there are some who want to feel happiness and are unable to obtain the feeling. That is when Western or Eastern medicine can be helpful. There are others who do not feel worthy to have joy in their life. They, too, need to reach out and find another who can assist them in their journey.

"Everyone deserves joy. It is my belief that God wants all people to be joyful. Joy is in the friendships one makes, the dog or cat welcoming them home, the kind word that has been spoken, the deeds we do for one another, or seeing the beauty that surrounds one.

"Joy is all around. Look!" she said excitedly, as she pointed to the trees. "One can learn much from trees. Look at those leaves; they are already starting to change color. They have lived a full cycle. In the spring, they sprouted new buds and grew new leaves and branches. They were trusting and growing. It was a time of new beginnings, much like each new day. The weather warmed; summer came. The leaves turned a rich green, blew in the wind, trusted *all would be well in the life journey. Autumn is now approaching. It is time for jubilation. The trees shout out for joy using bright colors, declaring the life journey is almost done. It is a sign they have lived and are not afraid of dying. The tree lets go of the leaves a little at a time until the tree becomes barren. Then it is time for the tree to rest and rejuvenate until the next beginning."*

"How do you seem to know and understand so much?" I asked.

Tree Spirited Woman had a twinkle in her eye as she said, *"One can be taught knowledge, but one can only gain wisdom when she is ready. The day will come that you, too, will know and understand. My life journey has been like that of the tree. I have learned to trust, and my seasons have been rich."*

Tree Spirited Woman looked at me; her face held a radiant glow. *"In your life, you must find and experience joy each day. That will be your gift to others."* She said this as if she wanted the message to penetrate deep into my soul.

I started to ask about her illness, but I stopped. It didn't seem appropriate at the moment. I vowed to myself I would ask her about it next month. We sat quietly, taking in the smells of drying leaves, hearing the sounds of birds singing, and feeling the calmness and joy that surrounded us.

Tree Spirited Woman took hold of both my hands and looked into my eyes. Watching the little flecks of gold dancing around her irises, I couldn't help but smile. She gently squeezed my hands and told me it was time for me to leave. She said she wanted to stay and enjoy some time alone.

Standing, looking down at Tree Spirited Woman, I felt so fortunate. My joy was for the present, for the time I had shared with Tree Spirited Woman, and for the changes that were happening within me. With tears in my eyes, I bent down, hugged Tree Spirited Woman, and said softly, "Thank you for sharing your knowledge and your wisdom with me." She held me tightly before letting go, and as I turned to walk away, I thought I heard her say, *"Good-bye Little One."* I quickly looked back, not sure I'd really heard anything. Tree Spirited Woman's eyes were closed, her face toward the sky, and the sun was shining down on her like a spotlight. I smiled to myself, turned, and continued down the path.

September 22

Summer is officially over, the leaves are already starting to change colors. In a few days, Tree Spirited Woman and I will have been meeting for a full year. As Tree Spirited Woman would say, one cycle has passed. Where has the time gone?

September 26

Today was a joy-filled day! I can't wait to tell Tree Spirited Woman all about it. I have agreed to marry again. I know I will continually need to work on letting go and trusting, but my life is worth it. I'm so excited to continue this life journey. So many possibilities!

Dear God, Thank you for everything! I feel so blessed.

FOURTEEN

Ending

Tree Spirited Woman didn't make our one-year anniversary. I waited in the woods for over two hours, but she didn't show. I knew she was sick, and my first thought was that something had happened to her. Then I became angry that she didn't have someone contact me to let me know what had happened. Still, I returned to the woods on the 28th for the next three months. She never reappeared.

The last time I was in the woods, I saw a hawk walking on the path ahead of me; it turned, looked at me, and then flew away. The hawk was reminding me to let go. I knew, then, that Tree Spirited Woman would never be back. I couldn't believe our time was over; I wasn't ready to let go. At that instant, a grief so overwhelming came upon me that I fell to my knees and sobbed. I didn't want to accept that she was gone.

I realized I only knew her as Tree Spirited Woman. I didn't know her real name or where she lived. We had met for almost a year, and I knew so little—and yet so much—about her.

For a while, I cried for the loss of the woman who had become my friend and my mentor. Then I celebrated her life, as I knew she would have wanted me to.

Tree Spirited Woman was right when she said she would always be a part of me. I am, in part, who I am because of knowing her. When I think of her wisdom and how she phrased her words, I feel calmness spread through me. Closing my eyes, I can still see her face, her twinkling eyes, with the flecks of gold that seemed to dance, and her embracing smile that filled my whole being.

Tree Spirited Woman told me to experience joy every day, and to share that gift with others. I try to honor her by doing just that. That's my way of thanking her. I don't let a day ever pass without looking around and seeing the goodness and the beauty that surrounds me. I never forget to say a thank you prayer for everything in my life, and, everyday, I make a conscious choice to be a positive person.

As I thought about her possible death, I had a reoccurring dream that Tree Spirited Woman and Grandmother were one. I wondered whether Tree Spirited Woman had been sent by my grandmother to share some of life's answers. Then I wondered whether Tree Spirited Woman was Grandmother, incarnate. I don't know. I just know that the time I spent with her was meant to be a part of my life journey, and for that I am forever grateful. Through Tree Spirited Woman, I gained much knowledge about myself and about life. It is from understanding this knowledge that I hope to gain her wisdom.

Tree Spirited Woman told me I needed to "let go and trust." It was through her teachings that I have come to believe in myself and to trust the voice within. As I was preparing to write this book, I quieted myself, let go of my emotions, and trusted the words would appear. The words have come from what I wrote in my grandmother's journal, and what my memory could recall. As Tree Spirited Woman would say, *"It is what is to be shared at this time."*

EPILOGUE

The cycle is now complete. You have heard the beginning, and have reached the ending. Tree Spirited Woman's words were meant to be shared, and putting my journal into book form has allowed me to share them with you. Take her words, learn from them, and find fulfillment in your life journey.

My wish for you is that you, too, learn to "let go and trust", and using Tree Spirited Women's words: *"In your life find and experience joy each day; that will be your gift to others."*

Discussion Questions

Beginning
- Talk about your relationship with your "Grandmother" or someone you think of as a Grandmother figure and share some of your memories.
- Who do you wish would have written to you prior to his or her death? Is there anyone to whom might like to write a letter?

Listening
- "Listening is a gift." Explain why you agree or disagree with this statement.
- Something to try: Next time you talk with someone, before you share anything about yourself, find out three new things about him or her.

Prayer
- How do you feel about prayer? Do you agree there is more than one way to pray?
- Imagine God is sitting next to you; what would you want to talk about?

Truth
- Do you believe there can be more than one truth to a story? Explain.
- Do you think there is ever a time when it's appropriate not to be truthful?

Relationships
- Think of three relationships you have in your life and explain what makes them important to you.
- Tree Spirited Woman says, "How one treats a stranger tells much about oneself." Discuss how you treat strangers.

Marriage
- "Marriage is when two people choose to love one another and commit to a lifelong relationship." Do you believe love is a choice? And do you believe marriage is for everyone? Explain.
- List five characteristics you believe make a good marriage?

Children
- What are some ways children influence you, and in what ways do you influence children?
- Imagine for one day you are a child again; how would you spend the day?

Menopause
- Do you agree menopause is something both men and woman go through? Why or why not?
- What are some things you will do for yourself when it is your time to travel through the stage of menopause?

Age
- "Age is but a number society puts on one to let them know when they are old." Do you agree with this? Explain.

Death
- You are in the time of living; is there anything you would want to change in your life? Explain. What's holding you back?
- Create a list of at least five things you would like others to remember about you when you're gone. Share what you've written.

Trust
- You really only have control over yourself; what are some things you try to change or control in others? Can you really make them change?
- List three things in your life that are blocking you from moving forward. Make a conscious choice to "let go and trust;" it is out of your control.

Joy!
- Share what you did today and list four things that were joyful. If you could pass on the gift of joy to one other person, who would that person be and why did you choose him or her?

Some things to think about
- Is it possible you have a person like Tree Spirited Woman in your life? Who might that be?
- Could you be that person for someone else?

ABOUT THE AUTHOR

Colleen Moran Baldrica is an official Chippewa (Ojibwe) Tribe member of the Pembina Band, from the White Earth Reservation in Northern Minnesota. She has worked for more than twenty years in public education, and holds advanced degrees with an emphasis in School Counseling. She lives in Stillwater, Minnesota, with her husband.

Tree Spirited Woman is the winner of a National Indie Excellence finalist book award in Spirituality, an Independent Publisher Book Award (IPPY) bronze medal winner in New Age: Mind, Body, and Spirit, and a finalist in the Best Books 2006 awards in Mind, Body, and Spirit.

For more information, visit **www.colleenbaldrica.com**.